This book belongs to:

_____

_____

For Reem, with love
I.T.

To Lily, with love Rosi
R.B.

HODDER CHILDREN'S BOOKS
First published in Great Britain in 2025
by Hodder and Stoughton

1 3 5 7 9 10 8 6 4 2

Text copyright © Isabel Thomas, 2025
Illustrations copyright © Rosalind Beardshaw, 2025

Isabel Thomas and Rosalind Beardshaw have asserted their right under
the Copyright, Designs and Patents Act 1988, to be identified
as the author and illustrator respectively of this work.
All rights reserved. A CIP catalogue record for this book
is available from the British Library.

HB ISBN 978-1-526-36562-0
PB ISBN 978-1-526-36563-7
E-book ISBN 978-1-444-98122-3

Printed in China

Hodder Children's Books
An imprint of Hachette Children's Group
Part of Hodder and Stoughton Limited
Carmelite House
50 Victoria Embankment
London, EC4Y 0DZ

An Hachette UK Company
www.hachette.co.uk
www.hachettechildrens.co.uk

The authorised representative in the EEA is Hachette Ireland,
8 Castlecourt Centre, Dublin 15, D15 XTP3, Ireland
(email: info@hbgi.ie)

Isabel Thomas Rosalind Beardshaw

Emily vs Gravity

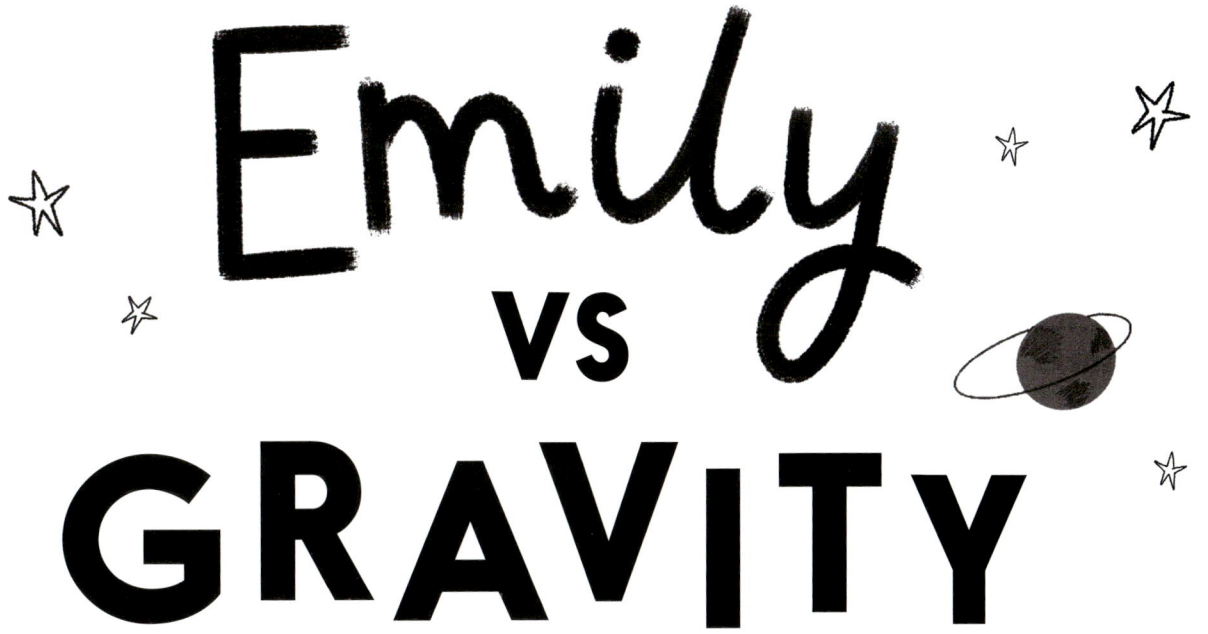

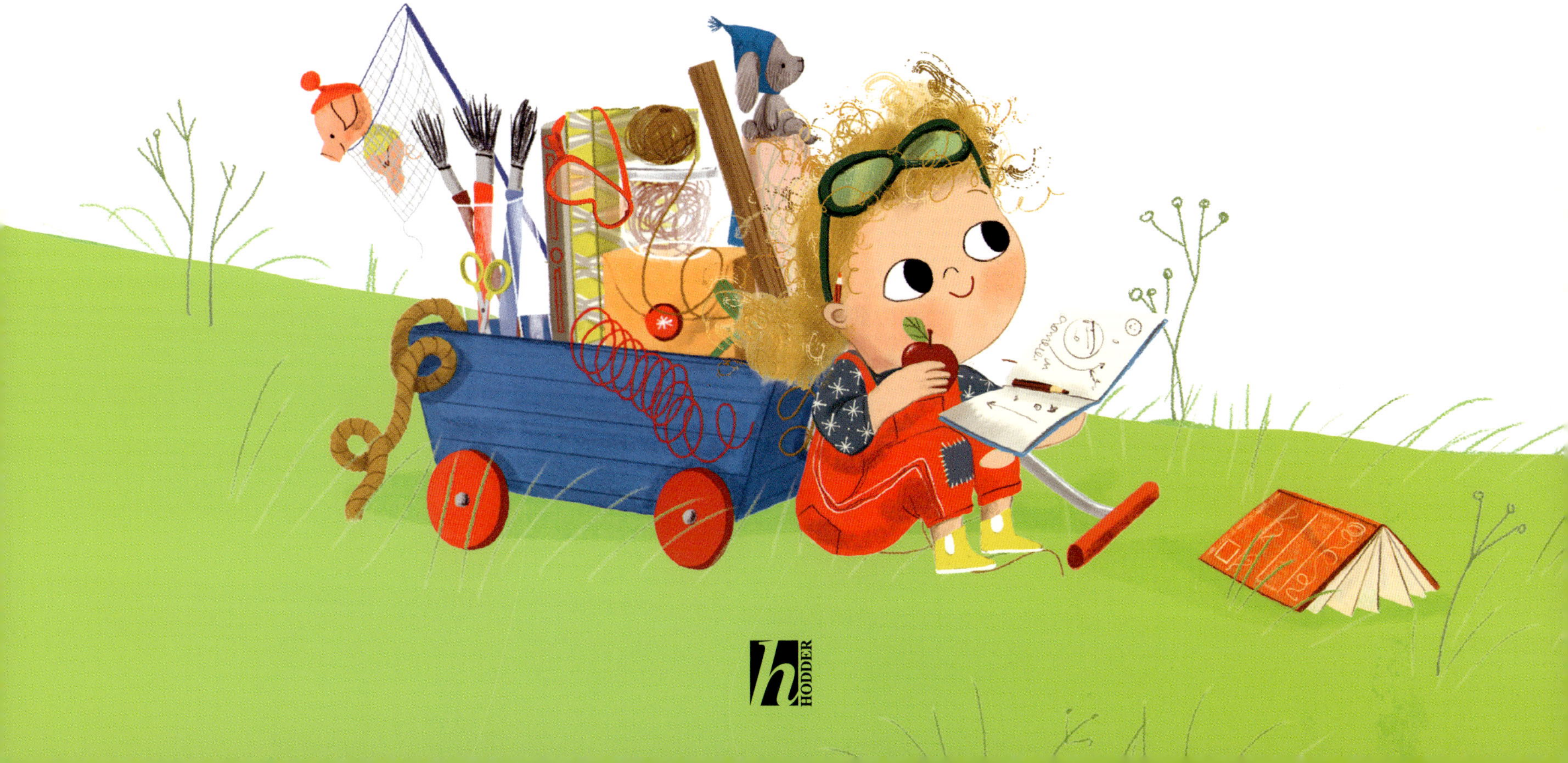

The battle began when Bear **fell** from the sky,

bounced twice

and **landed** at Emily's feet.

Bear stared up at the sky.

Emily decided to get Bear back where he belonged.

She threw Bear **UP**.

Emily knew that the best way to solve a big problem . . .

was to find a **BIG** book.

Emily discovered that to beat Gravity's **pull**,
she needed to give Bear a bigger **push**.
So, she balanced Bear on the seesaw

and quickly sat down
on the other end.

HOW GRAVITY WORKS

Gravity is a force that pulls things towards each other. The more massive an object is, such as a planet, the stronger it pulls on everything else. But gravity is weak compared to other forces. When you lift or throw something up, you are giving it a push big enough to beat gravity.

Birds beat Gravity every day.
So, Emily made Bear a pair of **wings**.

But birds can flap their wings and bears cannot.

So, Gravity pulled Bear . . .

It was time to try an **even BIGGER** book.

Emily learned that spacecraft don't need wings to stay up. Rockets launch them so fast, that Gravity's **pull** makes them travel in circles around the planet.

HOW SATELLITES STAY UP

Imagine a ball fired from a cannon. Pushed along by the cannon and pulled down by gravity, the ball falls in a curved path towards the ground. If the ball gets a bigger push, it travels faster and gets further before it hits the ground.

A satellite is launched with a rocket. By the time it reaches space, it is travelling at a very high speed and there is no air to slow it down. Like the cannon ball, the satellite continually falls, but its curved path stretches all the way around the planet in what we call an orbit.

Emily did not have a rocket.
So, she made a catapult.

With a **GIGANTIC** ping, Bear was launched into the air.

But as Bear pushed air out of the way, the air **pushed back** on Bear

and **slowed** him down.

Bear wasn't travelling as fast as a spacecraft. So, Gravity pulled him

straight . . .

back . . .

down.

A new idea appeared out of the blue
(as the best ideas do).

Emily packed Bear a sandwich,

fastened his harness and kissed him goodbye . . .

HOW BALLOONS STAY UP

A rubber duck in the bath pushes some water out of the way. The water pushes back. The upwards push from the water is greater than the downwards pull of gravity on the duck. The duck moves up.

A helium balloon works in the same way. It pushes air out of the way. The air pushes back. This push beats the pull of gravity on the balloon. The balloon moves up.

. . . then waved until he was just a speck.

Emily had beaten Gravity just in time for lunch.